Superfast
MOTORCYCLES

by Mark Dubowski

Consultant: Kim Barlag
Motorcycle Journalist and Historian

BEARPORT
PUBLISHING COMPANY, INC.

New York, New York

Credits

Cover, Courtesy of DaimlerChrysler; Title Page, Courtesy of DaimlerChrysler; 4, Courtesy of Grant Parson/Sam Wheeler; 5, Scott T. Smith/Corbis; 6, The Granger Collection, New York; 7, Courtesy of Honda Corporation; 8, Don Emde; 9, Minnesota Historical Society/Corbis; 10, AP Wide World Photos; 11, Don Emde; 12, Courtesy of Grant Parson/Sam Wheeler; 13, Courtesy of Grant Parson/Sam Wheeler; 14, Courtesy of Grant Parson/Sam Wheeler; 15, Courtesy of Dave Campos; 16-17, Courtesy of Grant Parson/Sam Wheeler; 18, Courtesy of Grant Parson/Sam Wheeler; 19, Courtesy of Grant Parson/Sam Wheeler; 20-21, Courtesy of Grant Parson/Sam Wheeler; 22, Courtesy of Kawasaki Company; 23, Alamy; 24, Courtesy of DaimlerChrysler; 25, Courtesy of Marine Turbine; 26, Scott T. Smith/Corbis; 27, Courtesy of Sam Wheeler; 29, Alamy.

Editorial development by Judy Nayer
Design & Production by Paula Jo Smith

Special thanks to Sam Wheeler for all his help

Library of Congress Cataloging-in-Publication Data

Dubowski, Mark.
  Superfast Motorcycles / by Mark Dubowski.
      p. cm.—(Ultimate speed)
  Includes bibliographical references and index.
  ISBN 1-59716-081-4 (library binding)— ISBN 1-59716-118-7 (pbk.)
  1. Motorcycles, Racing—History—Juvenile literature. I. Title. II. Series.

  TL442.D83 2006
  629.227′5—dc22

                              2005005335

For more information, write to Bearport Publishing Company, Inc., 101 Fifth Avenue, Suite 6R, New York, New York 10003. Printed in the United States of America.

1 2 3 4 5 6 7 8 9 10

CONTENTS

The Fastest Motorcycle in the World

Sam Wheeler started riding motorcycles when he was 13 years old. At first, he rode with his dad. Later, he rode with his friends. In August 2004, he was riding alone, on a racing test track.

Sam Wheeler's motorcycle looks more like a missile. Its shape helps it cut through the air and go as fast as a small jet.

Wheeler was riding a **streamliner**. These motorcycles help racers overcome one of their biggest problems— **wind resistance**. Streamliners have a smooth, curved covering. Their shape makes wind flow around the bike instead of pushing against the front of it.

Sam Wheeler thought his bike was the fastest motorcycle in the world. Now he was going to prove it. If he did, he would make motorcycle history.

Sam Wheeler tested his bike on the Bonneville Salt Flats, a dry lake bed in Utah. Here, riders can travel at top speed for a long distance, without turns to slow them down.

It Started with Bicycles

Motorcycle racing history started with bicycle racing. Riders trained for races by trying to keep up with the bike in front, called the pace bike.

A team of racers on a tandem motorcycle

Today, racers on bikes without **motors** can reach a speed of about 30 miles per hour (48 kph).

In 1898, Charles H. Metz invented a new and improved pace bike. He put a motor on a bicycle built for two people, called a tandem.

Metz used his invention to train bicycle racers. Riders sat in the front seat and pedaled to keep up with the motor. Riding Metz's motorized bicycle helped racers practice steady, fast pedaling.

Motorcycles have come a long way since 1898. The Super Blackbird is a very fast motorcycle built by Honda, a Japanese company. Its top speed is 186 miles per hour (299 kph).

Motorcycle Racing Is Born

Bicycle racers who saw Metz's motorized bike started to wonder: *How fast can we go on that?* So Charles Metz began to build motorbikes for racing as well as training. In the late 1800s, bicycle racetracks made of wood became the first racetracks for motorized bikes.

A wooden motorcycle racetrack in Springfield, Massachusetts

In 1899, Charles Metz became the first person to use the term "motor-cycle" instead of "motor-bicycle." The **engines** of these new machines were powerful for the time. People were used to riding horses that went 40 or 50 miles (64 or 80 km) a day. They thought a bike that went 40 or 50 miles per hour (64 or 80 kph) was truly amazing.

An early Harley-Davidson motorcycle, around the 1890s

In 1908, "Jake" DeRosier set a new motorcycle speed record by going 68.2 miles per hour (109.8 kph).

100 Miles Per Hour!

In 1909, the Coliseum in Los Angeles, California, opened. It was the first racetrack built just for motorcycle racing.

Huge crowds came to watch the races. Riders won money. Motorcycle racing was now a big sport.

Today, motorcycle racing is still a very popular sport. The World Superbike Championship features superfast bikes on racetracks with many turns.

These early racers were only going about 60 miles per hour (97 kph). This speed is slower than cars on today's highways. For 1909, however, it was fast.

Then, on December 30, 1912, a rider named Lee Humiston broke a big speed **barrier**. He became the first person ever to ride a motorcycle over 100 miles per hour (161 kph). His bike was called the Excelsior.

Lee Humiston was nicknamed "The Humiston Comet" after he became the first person to ride a bike over 100 miles per hour (161 kph).

The Takeoff

In 2004, it was Sam Wheeler's turn to break a speed record. He took his streamliner to the Bonneville Salt Flats. The ground there looks like it's covered with snow, but it's not. At one time it was under a lake. After the water dried up, a layer of salt was left on the ground. The salt makes the ground rough. This surface gives the tires extra **traction**.

The crew works on Sam Wheeler's streamliner.

Wheeler was strapped inside the **cockpit**. The crew lowered the cover. They pushed and ran alongside the bike.

Wheeler twisted the grip under his right hand. The engine roared, and the bike took off!

With Sam Wheeler strapped inside, the streamliner weighs about 1,044 pounds (474 kg).

"A Funny Noise"

Wheeler raced across the desert. All the while, he listened closely to the sound of the engine. Every sound it made told him something. It told him how the engine was doing, and when to **shift**.

Wheeler's streamliner on the Flats

Suddenly, the engine screamed. Sam Wheeler punched a button to shift the bike into second **gear**. The engine roared, then screamed again. Wheeler shifted into third. Every time Wheeler changed gears, the bike weaved a little. He turned the handlebars to keep the bike straight on track.

Then Wheeler heard something—"a funny noise." Something was wrong, but what was it?

Wheeler was trying to beat a 322-plus mile-per-hour (518-plus kph) record set by Dave Campos on the Harley-Davidson Easyriders Streamliner in 1990.

Dave Campos and his Easyriders Streamliner

The Last Mile

Sam Wheeler **accelerated**. He punched the shift button again and went into fourth gear. Then he punched it again, into fifth gear. Finally he was in sixth—the top gear, the top speed.

Red markers occur every 1/10 mile (.16 km) on the Salt Flats course. Yellow markers are placed every one mile (1.6 km).

The "funny noise" was still there. It wouldn't go away. What could it be? The engine seemed okay. It wasn't **overheating**. The mile markers were slipping by. The streamliner was going over 300 miles per hour (483 kph).

Sam Wheeler passed the four-mile marker. The end of the track was only a mile away. If the bike didn't crash or break, he could be there in 11 seconds.

The Finish Line

The streamliner screamed past the finish line. Sam Wheeler tapped the brakes and stopped. Crew members ran to him. They raised the cover and helped Wheeler out.

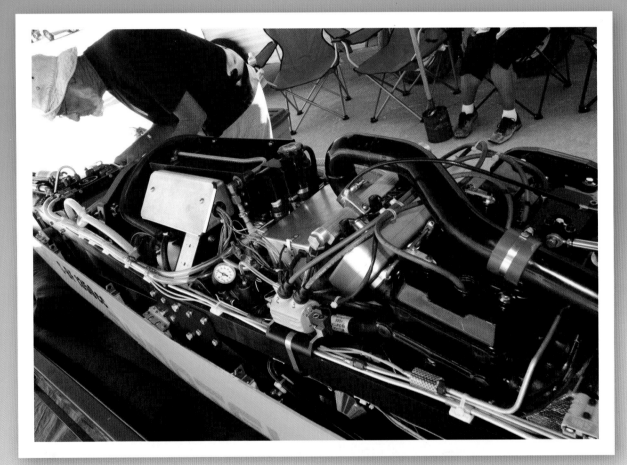

A crew member takes a look under the hood of the streamliner at a race in September 2004.

It took 8,500 hours to construct the streamliner.

However, the test wasn't over! The rules said the bike now had to make it back to the starting line. The **official** speed would be the **average** speed for both trips.

The crew looked at the engine and found that the "funny noise" was from a loose hose **clamp**. The crew easily fixed it. The next day, Sam Wheeler climbed into the streamliner for the race back to the starting line.

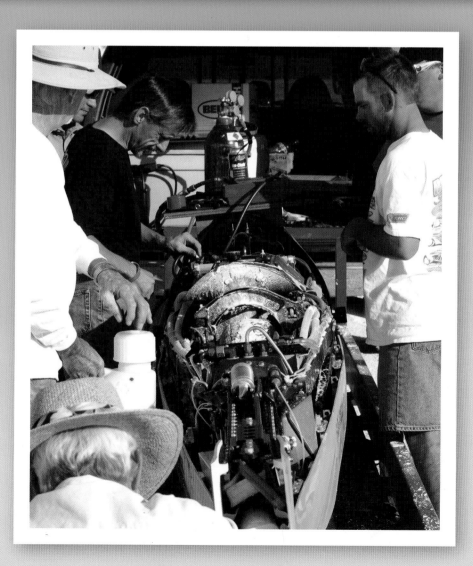

A World Record

On the first run, Wheeler's motorcycle had reached a top speed of 330.302 miles per hour (531.569 kph). The speed that counted, though, was the average speed for both runs. He started the bike up again and quickly raced back across the Flats. Wheeler shot across the starting line. Then he tapped the brakes, came to a stop, and looked through the **canopy**.

His crew was excited. They were shouting, hugging, and high-fiving. They had done it! Sam Wheeler's average speed was 332.410 miles per hour (534.962 kph). The E-Z Hook team had broken the world record by a little over one mile per hour (1.6 kph).

Sam Wheeler set the fastest record speed known for a two-wheeled vehicle.

Sam Wheeler's team at a race in September 2004

Rider: Sam Wheeler

E-Z-HOOK

Fast Bike for Sale

Sam Wheeler's motorcycle is not for driving on streets or highways. It is not for sale, either. However, some fast motorcycles are for sale. They are called production motorcycles.

The fastest production bike is the Suzuki Hayabusa (HYE-uh-boo-suh). Its top speed is 200 miles per hour (322 kph). The Hayabusa is a sportbike. On these kind of bikes, the rider leans forward to lower the wind resistance.

The Hayabusa was named after the Japanese falcon, a very fast bird. This bike can go from zero to 60 miles per hour (0–97 kph) in 2.5 seconds.

The Kawasaki Ninja ZX-12R

Not all production motorcycles are built for speed. One kind, called the classic style, is built for street riding and **touring**. Sitting upright, the rider can see all around.

A father rides a classic style bike along with his son who is on a toy motorcycle.

Too Fast for the Street

The fastest motorcycle ever built is the Dodge Tomahawk. The builders say the engine is strong enough for the bike to go 400 miles per hour (644 kph). Because of wind resistance, though, it cannot be ridden that fast.

The Dodge Tomahawk has an engine that is bigger and stronger than most car engines.

The Tomahawk is a concept bike. Concept bikes are not made to be sold. They are not even made for riding. The Tomahawk was made to give **engineers** new ideas about making better and faster motorcycles in the future.

The Tomahawk's 500-**horsepower** engine is the same engine used to power the Dodge Viper, a superfast car. The Tomahawk has four wheels, for extra traction.

Another superfast bike is the Y2K Turbine. It has an estimated top speed of 260 miles per hour (418 kph). It is much heavier and longer than regular sportbikes. People can buy the Y2K, but it is extremely expensive.

The Next World Record

It took Sam Wheeler 14 years to break the world record for speed on a motorcycle. He tried over and over again, with different bikes. Sometimes his bikes had engine trouble. Sometimes the tires blew out. Sometimes the wind was blowing the wrong way, making wind resistance an even bigger problem.

The Bonneville Salt Flats, where Sam set his world record, are near Utah's Great Salt Lake.

Wheeler never gave up. He kept on trying, year after year, until his efforts finally paid off.

How long until someone breaks the record again? Who will it be? Lots of people will try to beat the new world record. It might even be Wheeler, breaking his own record!

Sam Wheeler thinks his record will be broken someday. To do this, he believes a better tire needs to be invented to provide more traction on the salty ground.

JUST THE FACTS   More About Motorcycles

- The earliest motorcycles were mostly made of wood—even the wheels! The ride was so hard, people called these bikes "bone crushers."

- In 1909, a motorcycle was built with the engine at the bottom of the frame. Motorcycles have been built this way ever since.

- A helmet is the most important piece of safety gear for a motorcycle rider. It protects the head from brain injuries in the event of a crash. A helmet also cuts down wind noise, which makes it easier for riders to hear important sounds.

- Headlights make motorcycle riders more visible to automobile drivers. Some states make motorcycle riders use headlights even in daylight.

TIMELINE

This timeline shows some important events in the history of motorcycles.

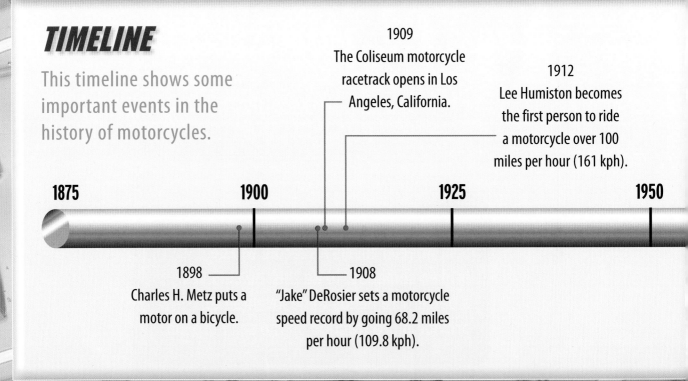

1909
The Coliseum motorcycle racetrack opens in Los Angeles, California.

1912
Lee Humiston becomes the first person to ride a motorcycle over 100 miles per hour (161 kph).

1875   1900   1925   1950

1898
Charles H. Metz puts a motor on a bicycle.

1908
"Jake" DeRosier sets a motorcycle speed record by going 68.2 miles per hour (109.8 kph).

- The famous stunt rider Evel Knievel did all his jumps on a Harley-Davidson.

- Yamaha, the Japanese company, used to make only musical instruments. It began making motorcycles after World War II.

- According to the *Guinness Book of World Records*, the longest motorcycle ride was a 101,322-mile (163,062-km) trip around the world. It took a team more than four years to finish.

- The world's smallest motorcycles are called minimotos, or pocket bikes. They look like toys, but adults race them at speeds of more than 60 miles per hour (97 kph).

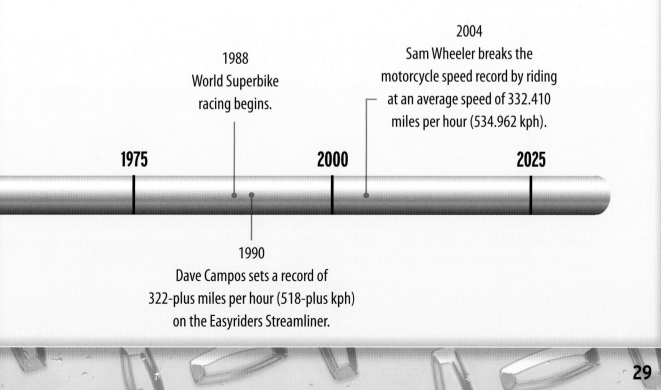

1988
World Superbike
racing begins.

2004
Sam Wheeler breaks the
motorcycle speed record by riding
at an average speed of 332.410
miles per hour (534.962 kph).

1975   2000   2025

1990
Dave Campos sets a record of
322-plus miles per hour (518-plus kph)
on the Easyriders Streamliner.

GLOSSARY

accelerated (ak-SEL-uh-*rate*-id) sped up; went faster

average (AV-uh-rij) in racing, the speed of a racer over the course of a race, including the time it takes to get started and reach top speed

barrier (BA-ree-ur) the end or top limit

canopy (KAN-uh-pee) a covering over the pilot

clamp (KLAMP) on a motorcycle, a metal band that holds a hose in place

cockpit (KOK-*pit*) the enclosed place where the driver sits

engineers (en-juh-NIHRZ) people who are trained to build machines, vehicles, roads, or other structures

engines (EN-juhnz) machines that cause motion

gear (GIHR) an adjustment that changes the speed of a motorcycle wheel compared to the speed of the engine

horsepower (HORSS-pou-ur) a unit for measuring an engine's power

motors (MOH-turz) machines that use power to make things move or work

official (uh-FISH-uhl) according to the rules

overheating (*oh*-vur-HEET-ing) when an engine becomes too hot and stops working

shift (SHIFT) to change gears

streamliner (STREEM-line-ur) a special type of motorcycle with a cover that helps the machine cut through the air

touring (TUR-ing) a motorcycle made for traveling long distances

traction (TRAK-shuhn) the gripping power that keeps a moving object from slipping on a surface

wind resistance (WIND ri-ZISS-tuhnss) the force of air that works against a fast-moving object

BIBLIOGRAPHY

greatsaltlake.utah.edu/

www.statnekov.com

www.streamliner.com

www.superblackbird.com

READ MORE

Graham, Ian. *Superbikes.* Chicago, IL: Heinemann Library (2003).

Jefferis, David. *Super Bikes.* Chicago, IL: Raintree (2001).

Kimber, David, and Richard Newland. *Motorcycle-Mania!* Milwaukee, WI: Gareth Stevens Publishing (2003).

Raby, Philip, and Simon Nix. *Motorbikes: The Need for Speed.* Minneapolis, MN: Lerner Publications Company (1999).

Sievert, Terri. *The World's Fastest Superbikes.* Mankato, MN: Capstone Press, Inc. (2002).

LEARN MORE ONLINE

Visit these Web sites to learn more about motorcycles:

www.ama-cycle.org

www.nationalmotorcyclemuseum.co.uk/

INDEX

ABOUT THE AUTHOR

Mark Dubowski is the author/illustrator of many books for young
readers. He rides a 1986 Kawasaki Vulcan 750.